Called to Be a Catechist

DISCOVERING DISCIPLESHIP

Inspiration and Professional Growth

TWENTY-THIRD PUBLICATIONS

twentythirdpublications.com

IMPRIMATUR

✛ Most Reverend
    Robert J. McManus, STD,
    Bishop of Worcester,
    February 23, 2018

TWENTY-THIRD PUBLICATIONS
One Montauk Avenue, Suite 200, New London, CT 06320
(860) 437-3012 » (800) 321-0411 » www.twentythirdpublications.com

Cover photo: © shutterstock / Syda Productions

ISBN: 978-1-62785-293-7
Library of Congress Catalog Card Number: 2017941586
Printed in the U.S.A.

A division of Bayard, Inc.

CONTENTS

INTRODUCTION 1

CHAPTER 1
Faith: A Lifetime Journey 3
Sr. Janet Schaeffler, OP

CHAPTER 2
Through Crises of Faith 10
Sr. Angela Ann Zukowski, MHSH

CHAPTER 3
Encountering Jesus 18
Most Reverend Charles Jason Gordon

CHAPTER 4
Words of Life-Giving Faith 27
William H. Johnston

CHAPTER 5
The Scriptures and Spirituality of Catechists 35
Fr. Donald Senior, CP

CHAPTER 6
Implementing the Catechism 42
Daniel S. Mulhall

CHAPTER 7
Mary: Disciple and Woman of Faith 49
Fr. Bertrand Buby, SM

ABOUT THE CONTRIBUTORS 57

RECOMMENDED RESOURCES 58

INTRODUCTION

Faith is an invitation, a gift; it is never forced. Faith is relational. We confess and live our faith in Jesus only as members of the believing community. Just as in our daily life we need one another, so, too, in our faith journey. We need the support of others to help us remain focused and on track.

Faith can be chaotic, challenging, and comforting. In his apostolic letter *The Door of Faith (Porta Fidei)*, Pope Benedict XVI declared a Year of Faith from October 2012 through November 2013, and called Catholics to rediscover their journey of faith in a more reinvigorating way so that it would "arouse in every believer the aspiration to *confess* the faith in fullness and with renewed conviction, with confidence and hope" (PF, n. 9). He says the task of every believer is "to rediscover the content of the faith that is professed, celebrated, lived and prayed..." (PF, n. 9).

This book will help you "rediscover the content of the faith," and will provide suggestions for personal formation and activities that can be used to emphasize the great gift of discipleship and the promise Jesus gave us, "If you remain in my word, you will truly be my disciples, and you will know the truth, and the truth will set you free" (John 8:31–32).

FAITH: *A* LIFETIME JOURNEY

SR. JANET SCHAEFFLER, OP

*Is faith one of those words we use often, not realizing the depth
of its meaning? Could we ever realize its expanse?*

There is much to say and reflect on regarding this mystery—
faith. The Prologue and Part One of the *Catechism of the
Catholic Church* explore topics such as "Handing on the Faith:
Catechesis," "The Interpretation of the Heritage of Faith," "The
Obedience of Faith," "The Characteristics of Faith," "The Language of Faith,"
etc. A Bible concordance reveals 447 passages in Scripture about faith.

In many ways, we could make several distinctions of faith or look at
faith through different lenses and, through each, see a new facet.

Faith and the Act of Faith

There is a difference between faith and the act of faith. "Faith" is a gen-
erous invitation from our loving God to each and every human person.
This is a personal invitation to enter into an intimate, loving relationship with God, an invitation that never forces but always surrounds us
with love and urging.

The "act of faith" is our response to this invitation, this gift. Saint Augustine prayed, "You have made us for yourself, O Lord, and our hearts are restless until they rest in you." We, as humans, are always searching; we are incomplete. Faith is God's gift, God's invitation to relationship, so that we may be filled with the life and love of God.

Because God is all-loving, because God created us free, and because faith is an invitation and a gift, it is never forced. The act of faith is our response; it comes from our search for our completeness; it is our response to God's gift of love, life, and relationship. As a result, faith is about much more than an assent in our minds to beliefs and truths about God, the Trinity, the church, and various teachings. It is an encounter with God; it is a relationship. Faith is alive. It is growing. It is never the same from day to day. It is a lifelong journey.

Three Dimensions of Faith

In some ways, we can understand our lifelong journey of faith as encompassing three dimensions: intellectual faith, relational faith, and practicing (or active) faith.

Intellectual faith

Our "intellectual faith" might be the first that comes to mind: that body of truths that we know, that we know about, that we can articulate. This is crucial to who we are and whose we are. As Catholic Christians, we profess our intellectual faith each Sunday in the Creed. This is further nurtured as we continue to learn, in lifelong formation, about what it is that grounds us as disciples of Jesus, the Christ.

Each Sunday we pray, "I believe." In the early church, *credo* was the verb form of the noun *faith*. The dictionary definition of *believe* is "to have confidence in the truth or the reliability of something, although without absolute proof that one is right in doing so." Often, when we pray the Creed today, then, we transfer that definition so that we presume we're praying, "I give my assent to."

That is true, but it goes far beyond that. The Latin roots of the word combine to mean "I give my heart to." The heart is where we are most truly ourselves, more so than in our intellect. In the giving of our heart, *credo* means "I commit my loyalty to." When we pray "credo" at the beginning of the Creed, we are saying "I give my heart to God."

The pre-modern meanings of the word *believe* also go deeper than just the intellect. Prior to the seventeenth century, the word *believe* did not mean believing in the truth of statements or propositions. Grammatically, the object of believing was not statements but a person. The contexts in which it was used in pre-modern English made it clear that it was all about persons: to hold dear, to prize, to give one's loyalty, to give one's self to, to commit one's self. Most simply, *to believe* meant "to love."

In fact, the English words *believe* and *belove* (beloved) are related. What we believe is what we belove. To believe in someone is to belove that person. To be a disciple of Jesus is all about believing in him and all that he beloves. Intellectual faith is more than just facts and doctrines!

Relational faith

Thus, the second dimension of our lifelong faith journey, "relational faith," flows naturally and is interrelated and interconnected to the first. It's all that was described at the opening of the article: Relational faith is an invitation from our loving God, a divine

> Our relational faith is our personal response, yet it is an act linked to the faith of others. We never do it alone.

gift, a grace from God that enables us to make an authentic human act of faith. We respond to God's loving gift.

The centrality of faith as our relationship with God is clear as we—catechists—are continually reminded of the goal of catechesis: "The definitive aim of catechesis is to put people not only in touch, but also in communion and intimacy, with Jesus Christ" (*General Directory for Catechesis*, n. 80). The *Catechism of the Catholic Church* (CCC) likewise reminds us, "Catechesis aims at putting 'people…in communion…with

Jesus Christ: only he can lead us to the love of the Father in the Spirit and make us share in the life of the Holy Trinity'" (n. 426).

Our relational faith is our personal response, yet it is an act linked to the faith of others. We never do it alone. An anonymous Christian is an oxymoron. The *Catechism of the Catholic Church* reminds us: "faith is not an isolated act. No one can believe alone, just as no one can live alone. You have not given yourself faith as you have not given yourself life…I cannot believe without being carried by the faith of others…" (n. 166).

Practicing (or active) faith

Perhaps the best way to understand "practicing (or active) faith" is through asking ourselves two questions: Inside what commitments am I sitting? Within what reality do I anchor myself?"

Practicing (or active) faith completes our intellectual and relational faith. Each is needed; each builds upon the other. We can't bypass or eliminate one. The gospel challenges us to be aware of the third dimension of faith: to continually look at what we are doing and how we are living. Perhaps to remind us of our practicing/active faith, an added beatitude for us today would be "Blessed are those who hear the word of God and live it."

This Lifetime Journey

The incredible reality that faith is a journey that lasts a lifetime leaves us appreciating that our faith journey can be chaotic, challenging, and comforting.

Chaotic

In the past few decades, there has been much "discovered" about chaos theory, the very complex way the world works. We need only return to Genesis 1:2: "the earth was without form or shape, with darkness over the abyss and a mighty wind sweeping over the waters."

The beginnings, described in Genesis, are often echoed in our lives of darkness, emptiness, tossing, and churning. Chaos, however, is not detrimental for those on the journey of faith, for those who see with the eyes of faith, for those in relationship with the One who offers faith.

What can happen in these chaotic times for those who respond to the gift of faith? Do the gentle winds of faith console? Do the fresh winds of faith support? Do the powerful winds of faith energize?

> The incredible reality that faith is a journey that lasts a lifetime leaves us appreciating the fact that our faith journey can be chaotic, challenging, and comforting.

Challenging

The lifelong journey of faith is not a complacent one; it is not one that can be taken for granted or be put on the back burner. Because faith is fundamentally a relationship—as are all bonds—it must be nurtured.

Each of faith's three dimensions (intellectual, relational, and practicing/active) needs continual tending. Friends in close relationship strive to know more and more about each other; lovers can't learn enough. This describes the reality of intellectual faith. In many ways, the challenge of constant and ongoing learning in faith is made easy today because children, youth, and adults of all ages and needs are surrounded by creative and faith-filled opportunities to continue growing in faith.

Relational faith is nurtured through daily presence, such as prayer and meditation, the celebration of the sacraments, and recognizing God in everyday life and ordinary moments.

Nurturing the dimension of practicing/active faith is a challenge—and a mandate—that flows from our baptismal promises. It's who we are. Saint John Chrysostom reminds us, "The sincerity of our prayer is determined by our willingness to work on its behalf." In faith, we are called to be what we have promised in baptism: to live our prayers.

Comforting: In this fast-food, easily disposable culture, we are privileged to be on a journey of faith that is lifelong, permanent, enduring, and constant. We have been invited into a relationship with our God, who loves unconditionally, cares completely, and forgives unceasingly.

Your Thoughts

1 Saint Augustine wrote: "You have made us for yourself, O Lord, and our hearts are restless until they rest in you." How does his prayer resonate in my life today?

_____

_____

_____

2 In my journey of faith, what is/has been chaotic, challenging, and comforting?

_____

_____

_____

Try This

Develop a timeline of your journey of faith thus far. Have there been twists, turns, construction points, and detours? Reflect on your timeline with regard to what you came to understand about your personal journey of faith.

THROUGH CRISES
of FAITH

SR. ANGELA ANN ZUKOWSKI, MHSH

Entering my office, the student broke down in tears and proclaimed with deep emotion, "I am having a crisis of faith! My parents are upset with me. They believe I have lost my faith. I feel like I am lost in a kind of desert. Help me!"

As a professor in a Catholic university, one encounters the rollercoaster ride of our students' maturing faith life. There is no doubt that when a young person leaves the safe haven of his or her home environment and enters the world of serious academia—with its religious and cultural diversity and cacophony of religious attitudes or dispositions—questions arise that can lead to an inner awakening for redefining a personal relationship with Jesus and the church. This is normal! For some young people, this is a desert experience.

Navigating the Experience

Some students may feel their spiritual lives being shaken when the black-and-white answers of the past collide with a diversity of religious perspectives. Some react against the religious life they have come to believe because they perceive that it isn't really religious but "supernaturalistic"—a religious life not connected with their lived experience but a kind of superstructure that does not speak to their present situation. Others discover that their new freedom to explore other traditions is a fresh, religious awakening with questions never before posed in their religious formation.

While some parents may panic, we realize this time may not be a real crisis of faith but rather an opportunity for the young person to reconfirm what he or she believes from a deeper, more informed, and personal perspective. It may not seem an easy path to navigate unless one has the spiritual support of a campus ministry team, present and attentive 24/7.

There are students, however, who desire to navigate through their experiences alone or with a few friends or by connecting through select faith blogs, chat rooms, Facebook, or more. If these alternative faith dialogue partners are grounded in a profound relationship with Jesus, students have a solid platform for their struggles with ambiguities. If not, their struggles can only deepen and become more complex because of the haziness, ignorance, or limited faith commitment of the dialogue partners.

Those of us who serve as catechists, parish spiritual leaders, mentors, and guides need to pursue our own spiritual, catechetical, biblical, and theological formation to be able to address the questions, struggles, and ambiguities that our young people bring to us. This is not a time to waffle with weak responses that have not been tested within our own desert experiences. We are called to be salt and light for all those who seek to come out of the desert.

Crises of Faith Today?

In his apostolic letter *The Door of Faith* (PF), Pope Benedict XVI writes: "Whereas in the past it was possible to recognize a unitary cultural matrix, broadly accepted in its appeal to the content of the faith and the values inspired by it, today this no longer seems to be the case in larger swathes of society, because of a profound crisis of faith that has affected many people" (n. 2).

Pope Benedict pointed out the many concerns within our secular cultural context that distract us from being "fully conscious of the grave difficulties of the time, especially with regard to the profession of the true faith and its correct interpretation" (PF, n. 5). Let's spend some time reflecting on this reality to grasp its breadth and depth.

We should not be afraid to face the problems of faith that are emerging around us. Nevertheless, are we prepared to do this? Perhaps we have become too comfortable with simplistic answers to complex spiritual realities. Perhaps we have not allowed ourselves quality contemplative reading, study, and reflection to capture the breadth and depth of religious knowledge and contextual understanding to face the faith challenges of the twenty-first century. Yet, faith has to be rethought within contemporary circumstances.

Now, more than ever, our vision of the world, of humanity, of anthropology—even diverse anthropologies and visions of humanity—are challenging us each and every day. We experience this when we are faced with the vast political issues that call for stances of faith that defend and respect the dignity of the human person. Media have created a world of nanosecond communication with a cacophony of religious and spiritual opinions, perspectives, and behaviors. The acceleration of change in cultural and social life is becoming a trigger igniting queries about the relationship of faith and life, the relationship of faith and reason, and the interpretation of faith for being authentically human in a changing world.

There is no doubt that to believe is a risky adventure. Yet we need not be alarmed. Our times call for a profound and mature faith, a faith that is courageous in the face of copious questions and challenges arising from our students' lived experiences, a faith that is willing to listen faithfully by listening deeply to the questions beneath the stated questions or comments to discover the movements of the Holy Spirit. This is our catechetical task.

To Speak of "Faith"

Fr. Gustavo Gutierrez wrote: "in the first place, let's say that to speak of 'faith' is an abstraction. What exists in reality are people who believe, people who have a faith, that is, people who accept the word of the Lord." The center of faith is the conviction that God comes to the world by means of Jesus Christ—not as an abstract God, a philosophical God, a conceptual God, but an active revelation of God. By prayerfully reading and meditating on the gospel stories and New Testament accounts of the faith of the early Christian communities, we come to know who Jesus is and what Jesus calls us to become. We discover that our hearts are burning with a deep desire to embrace the path of discipleship, the Jesus way of life that leads to beatitude living.

> The center of faith is the conviction that God comes to the world by means of Jesus Christ—not as an abstract God, a philosophical God, a conceptual God, but an active revelation of God.

Jürgen Moltmann once called attention to the danger of "little faith," or the dwarfing of faith. He understood "little faith" to be found where people were afraid of freedom and lacked courage, were suspicious of one another and the world, and were willing to stand back and not embrace a more robust and intentionally lived faith. Those with "little faith" seem to abandon the faith; thus, we may hear "I am going to leave the church and explore another religion" or "Everyone I know seems to be abandoning religion all together and embracing a more personal, individual spirituality." In this spirit, those with "little faith" sense that only a small remnant of the faithful will remain in the future. Perhaps this attitude is what most threatens faith today.

Risks, Relevancy, and Identity

Cardinal Joseph Ratzinger (Pope Benedict XVI) frequently wrote about the many risks of having faith in the modern world. He saw a danger that faith could retreat before the world so as to feel secure within itself, so that it cannot be attacked by anyone.

Or, an opposite yet also dangerous position could be that one sees how mere piety uprooted from the world is useless and that faith lived in the church does not correspond to the call for living and witnessing the Gospel within our immediate cultural contexts. In this context, faith becomes a purely political activity. Here faith can become secularized, losing its face and identity.

We find recent church documents articulating a double crisis of faith: the crisis of relevance and the crisis of identity. The crisis of relevance is sown in the fact that many Christians today don't know why they should believe or how faith could change their lives. It seems as though, for many, to believe or not to believe—in a Christian sense—would change nothing in their lives, so why believe? Yet, if we strive to make the church more relevant in society, we risk being engaged in the church from a simple human perspective—not from a faith perspective. So what difference does faith make?

Here people begin to fall into the crisis of identity. We begin to hear people ask, "Why am I a Christian?" "Why do I need faith?" "Can't I live the Beatitudes perhaps even more assertively than those who state they believe in a beatitude way of life yet don't witness to it?" An authentic conversion to Jesus Christ opens the door of faith. If our faith is concentrated in the person of Jesus Christ, we become disciples who concentrate deeply on the origin of faith, on Christ himself.

But what do we understand when we say or imply the word *God* and/or *Jesus* in our conversations? Have these words become like "ciphers" that no longer say or mean anything to our contemporary world? This is why Pope Benedict invited catechists to be new missionaries in a new age. He called us "to rediscover the joy of believing and the enthusiasm for communicating the faith. In rediscovering [God's] love day by day, the missionary commitment of believers attains force and vigor that can never fade away. Faith grows when it is lived as an experience of love received and when it is communicated as an experience of grace and joy" (PF, n. 7).

Catechetical Approaches

As catechists, we need to identify new methodologies to reformulate how we communicate faith in these changing times. This is not an option! It is a serious mandate rooted in our Catholic tradition. We need to recover Christian values that are at the heart of Catholicism and speak to modern times while remaining grounded in the richness of our Tradition.

> We need to reach our young people with a faith that proclaims truly Good News.

We need to reach our young people with a faith that proclaims truly Good News. All too often the Good News comes out as an ideology or theological construct that is restrictive in regards to salvation and not redeeming grace. Yet Christianity is about great joy! The word *joy* can be found more than 256 times in Scripture, and Pope Benedict XVI frequently spoke about joy for reinvigorating faith within our faith communities.

In the beautiful post-synodal apostolic exhortation titled *Word of God (Verbum Domini)*, the Holy Father desired to "point out certain fundamental approaches to a rediscovery of God's word in the life of the Church as a wellspring of constant renewal" and hopes that "the word will be ever more fully at the heart of every ecclesial activity" (n. 1).

By studying this document in one hand and the Scriptures in the other, catechists are enriched with the power of the word to inspire, motivate, and encourage students to come out of the desert courageously and enter the door of faith that offers the fullness of life. We help them understand that the Scriptures are the living word that speaks of the presence of God in our lives and the world today. Within the Scriptures, we draw living waters that heal, refresh, and give new life.

Our Task Today

Pope Benedict XVI believed that the future of the church depends on forming concrete, visible communities that are profound and vital witnesses to the Christian experience. These small communities (parishes) will reflect a new way of being dynamic, living, prophetic communities of faith.

Yet, these small communities should not lose their catholic (universal) character; they should not stand alone and degenerate into sects and cease to be churches. This could be the danger! We see these same thoughts reiterated in *The Door of Faith*, as Benedict encouraged us to strive to rediscover ways to incarnate and make our faith communities into living encounters with Christ.

Our primary task today is to rediscover our faith, cultivate a dynamic living faith community, and welcome and embrace those from desert experiences into a community of living waters.

Your Thoughts

1 What are my greatest fears when I think about someone coming to me with their faith crisis? Why?

_____

_____

2 Do I see the crises of relevance and identity in my life? In the life of my students? In my family? In my parish? What does it look like? How do I address it?

_____

_____

_____

Try This

Using the timeline of your journey of faith from the last chapter, consider one of the times you may have had a desert experience. What were the feeling, sense, or thoughts that were associated with it? Did you share the experience with anyone, and if so, with whom? Was the sharing helpful?

3

ENCOUNTERING JESUS

MOST REVEREND CHARLES JASON GORDON

*On January 10, 2012, Jefferson Bethke uploaded his "Spoken Word"
on YouTube: "Why I Hate Religion but Love Jesus" (youtube.com/
watch?v=1IAhDGYlpqY). It went viral. As of this writing, it has received
more than twenty-nine million hits. If you have not seen it, I recommend
you do so before reading this chapter.*

A video goes viral because it sparks something in the unconscious. There are cultural clues imbedded in this video that
resonate deeply with the generation that Bethke belongs to
and now represents.

It is important for catechists to realize how different generations
imbed and interpret cultural clues. This enables us to engage in creative discourse (conversation) with what is being communicated and by
whom. For example, Bethke is of Generation Y (born between 1980 and
2000), often referred to as Millennials.

People of this generation are confident, reflect high expectations, and
are not afraid to question societal norms or authority. They are the true
online natives and have integrated technology into their everyday lives.
Technology forms a major part of their entertainment and socializing.
They are somewhat conventional but still powerful.

Generation Y differs from the Traditionalist Generation (born between 1925 and 1945), the Baby Boomer Generation (born between 1946 and 1964), and Generation X (born between 1965 and 1979). Each has a particular perspective on the meaning of life and their roles and contributions for living full lives. It is imperative for us as catechists to come to terms with these differences if we are to interpret the spoken word that communicates an imbedded message.

This video, I believe, is the statement of a generation trying to grapple with the fundamentals of Christianity and coming down on the side of encountering Jesus as essential. This is not only in America; this video also went viral in Barbados, St. Vincent, and Trinidad. I am reading the text the way Carl Jung would read a dream—not literally but for the breaking forth of the unconscious into conscious life.

The church must position itself to engage not only the older generations but the emerging generations that are asking different questions and have different expectations.

The BIG Idea from Bethke

Bethke says that Jesus hates religion because religion is filled with hypocrisy; because religion does not get to the core, it does not deal with my moral shortcoming; because religion is a museum for good people not a hospital for the broken; because religion is not a conduit for grace.

So, Bethke says, Jesus and religion are opposite clans.

In this video there are straight shots at institutional religion. The sentiments are now far more mainstream than we would like to believe. In a recent Pew Research Poll, 27% of Americans are saying that they are spiritual not religious. Big religion is not where this generation is finding its spiritual home. They are looking for a more direct encounter with Jesus as a way of expressing their souls.

In his second stanza, Bethke says:

> They can't fix their problems and so they just mask it,
> not realizing religion's like spraying perfume on a casket.

See, the problem with religion is it never gets to the core.
It's just behavior modification, like a long list of chores,
like let's dress up the outside, make it look nice and neat.
But it's funny that's what they used to do to mummies
while the corpse rots underneath.

In the New Testament, Jesus is in conflict with certain social groups. His condemnation of the scribes and Pharisees, for example, is legendary. The condemnation is because of hypocrisy (see Luke 11:37–54). Jesus even warns his disciples to "beware of the leaven of the Pharisees and Sadducees" (Matthew 16:6). The disciples do not understand; they have no sight; they have no perception (see Matthew 16:9).

If Jesus is against something, it is not religion; it is hypocrisy. The encounter with Jesus is only real if it leads to a confrontation of hypocrisy in ourselves first—and then in the church. Many in the Traditionalist and the Baby Boomer generations seem to have become complacent and accommodating to hypocrisy—living by the rules of the market economy during the week and by another set of rules on Sunday.

But Generation Y is not so complacent and accommodating. In fact, some in this generation have a great intolerance. This is apt for the developmental stage. But in this generation, it is also a hallmark. If there is to be any renewal, we need Generation Y at all levels of church. We need their energy, their idealism, their insight, their commitment to serve the planet and humanity, and their desire to encounter Christ. They will help us grow a healthy intolerance for hypocrisy in ourselves and in our church.

Encountering Jesus

Behind this criticism of religion, there is the collective—and yes, unconscious—aspiration that Bethke's video contains. Here center stage is a desire for encountering Jesus. It is not behavior modification but getting to the core and dealing with our weakness. It is finding the path that St. Paul found, where he would boast of his weakness (see 2 Corinthians

12:1–10). It is coming to the place where the hypocrisy is no longer a parallel existence to the religious identity—living one thing on Saturday night and another on Sunday morning. It is not simply following the rules; rather, it is a deep, abiding encounter with the One who offers us grace.

> "If grace is water, the Church should be an ocean."
> **JEFFERSON BETHKE**

The yearning here is for grace. "If grace is water, the Church should be an ocean," says Bethke. Not grace just in the encounter with Christ, but grace in the encounter with his church as well.

Let us define grace as God's unmerited gift or favor. The yearning is that anyone coming to church would encounter grace in abundance through the people, the ministers, the priest, and those in leadership. This is not an unrealistic expectation. It is the central challenge. If the church is not an ocean of grace for those in need of mercy, then we have failed to be mature disciples of Christ. We have failed to understand Christ. What is worse, we have failed to keep the dangerous memory of Christ alive—which was his command to us (see Luke 22:19).

Many of the Baby Boomer Generation and the Traditionalist Generation may have no idea what it is like to grow up in and be deeply immersed in and influenced by a visual culture. In the post-sexual-revolution era, young people experience pornography and sex—seen through the lens of the dominant culture—as recreational sport on their phones and computers. If we do not understand the spiritual impact of these very important differences between the years of our own youth and what the youth of today experience, we will not be able to lead this generation to an encounter with Christ through their weaknesses.

This is about grace and human weakness. We come to this only through an understanding of our own weaknesses and the unmerited gifts that God has given us in calling us sons and daughters. This is what St. Paul refers to when speaking of the thorn in his side (see 2 Corinthians 12:7–10). This is the existential truth of the human condition.

Encountering Jesus: Biblical Witness

Christianity stands or falls based upon the encounter with the risen Lord. The New Testament gives us several paths to understand this encounter. Many of the accounts have a common pattern: A person is present but not recognized; there is something (a Christological key) that unlocks the blindness; those present recognize Christ and then reflect upon their experience.

For example, Mary of Magdala presumes Jesus to be the gardener until he calls her by name. Then her eyes are opened and she encounters Christ (see John 20:11–18). Thomas refuses to believe until he is invited to put his hand into the wounds of Christ (see John 20:24–29). The disciples walking to Emmaus recognize the stranger who accompanies them only in the breaking of the bread (see Luke 24:13–35). Peter recognizes Jesus in the abundance of the catch and is then commissioned to feed Jesus' lambs and sheep and to follow him (see John 21:1–19).

> It is their [early Christians'] encounter with the resurrected Christ, followed by the Pentecost experience, that transforms the early church.

Without these encounters and Christological keys, the early church would not have left the safety of the upper room to venture fearlessly into discipleship, proclaiming Jesus as the risen Lord. They saw Jesus but they did not recognize him until their eyes were opened. I dare say the Christians of today may also be encountering Christ without recognizing him, thus living by the rule and the law and not by the grace of the resurrection and Pentecost.

A true encounter with Christ will lead to deep conversion: sustaining prayer, forgiveness of ourselves and others, and gratitude to God and others for the rich blessings we have received without merit. Ultimately, an encounter with Christ will lead to hospitality—to welcoming all as brothers and sisters regardless of race, class, gender, or creed. This welcome will have a special place for the poor and marginalized.

Hearing ourselves called by name, touching the wounds of Christ, entering into the Eucharist, and responding to our commission are the spiritual paths that the Evangelists left for us to encounter the risen Christ. These paths are not for those living only in apostolic times. Rather, they are for Christians of all times. They are supposed to be the foundation of our Christianity.

Without the encounter with Jesus, the New Testament church would have remained disempowered and afraid of the hostile environment. It is their encounter with the resurrected Christ, followed by the Pentecost experience, that transforms the early church. Yet, many of us today believe that we can be Catholic without encountering Christ. We are fast approaching what Fr. Karl Rahner, SJ, predicted when he proposed that Christianity of the future will be mystical or not at all.

Catechetical Initiatives

If Generation Y is seeking an authentic encounter with Christ, then our parishes and catechetical programs need to be rethought. I offer two pastoral initiatives that could make a difference.

First, we need to find ways for the liturgy to be a sacred space for encountering Christ. We have become accustomed to the Mass. The familiarity sometimes has meant that we do not do the work and preparation necessary to ensure the Mass is the premier place for the encounter with Christ.

The *Constitution on the Sacred Liturgy (Sacrosanctum Concilium)* states:

> To accomplish so great a work, Christ is always present in his church, especially in her liturgical celebrations. He is present in the sacrifice of the Mass, not only in the person of his minister, "the same one now offering, through the ministry of priests, who formerly offered himself on the cross," but especially under the Eucharistic species. (SC, n. 7)

The article concludes: "From this it follows that every liturgical celebration, because it is an action of Christ the priest and of his Body which is the Church, is a sacred action surpassing all others; no other action of the Church can equal its efficacy by the same title and to the same degree." Yet, many Catholics do not experience the manifold presence of Christ in their Sunday liturgy. The priest and everyone in liturgical ministry need to work together so that the liturgy becomes an expression of God's grace and the privileged place of encounter.

The second initiative of this generational challenge is to the whole enterprise of catechesis. Catechists need to listen to the intergenerational discourse. We need our catechetical programs to be rooted in a genuine encounter with Jesus.

For example, the mystical tradition and traditional forms of prayer are integral to catechesis of all ages, especially to the young. Our young people need to encounter Christ as part of their journey of discipleship and to be initiated into the mysteries and rich inner life where prayer and silence are everyday experiences. When that encounter is reached through a life of prayer, listening, and discernment, only then will our youth give themselves fearlessly to Christ. Pope Benedict XVI proposed that faith is not only for living faithfully with Christ; it is also the foundation for interpreting humanity and human living.

Faith and Charity

Pope Benedict XVI reaffirmed what Pope Paul VI said, that integral human development is the vocation of the church (see Pope Benedict's 2009 encyclical letter *Charity in Truth [Caritas in Veritate]*, n. 16ff). For Pope Paul VI, the highest levels of development require "faith—God's gift to men of good will—and our loving unity in Christ" (*The Development of Peoples [Populorum Progressio]*, n. 21; Pope Pius VI, 1967). Yet, our catechetical programs very often do not address the real developmental needs of our children.

We need to address human, spiritual, moral, and physical developmental needs. This includes giving children a love of and commitment to the development of others, especially the poor. A true encounter with Christ leads to authentic development of the whole person. We cannot expect anything less, nor can we offer anything less to this generation.

Benedict XVI concluded his apostolic letter *The Door of Faith* by stating: "Faith without charity bears no fruit, while charity without faith would be a sentiment constantly at the mercy of doubt. Faith and charity each require the other, in such a way that each allows the other to set out along its respective path" (n. 14).

Your Thoughts

1. What is my attitude or disposition about hypocrisy as I strive to live and express my faith life?

_____

_____

2. How do I understand the meaning of grace? What insights do I glean from this chapter that invite a deeper appreciation for grace in my life?

_____

_____

Try This

In his apostolic letter *The Door of Faith*, Pope Benedict XVI wrote: "Today...there is a need for stronger ecclesial commitment to new evangelization in order to rediscover the joy of believing and the enthusiasm for communicating the faith" (n. 7). What new specific approach would make a difference in your parish or catechetical classroom? Design a catechetical plan of action to accomplish it.

WORDS *of* LIFE-GIVING FAITH

WILLIAM H. JOHNSTON

Christian creeds articulate in concise, almost poetic form some of the most fundamental of the saving and joyful truths that constitute the Christian faith.

Early twentieth-century British author Evelyn Underhill (d. 1941) began one of her many writings on mysticism and spirituality by recounting that "a very earnest but rather nebulous lady once defined her creed to me in these words: 'I feel there is a spiritual something somewhere.'"

Well, that's a start. And, indeed, it represents a not uncommon way of understanding things shared by people today ("I'm spiritual, not religious") as well as in New Testament times—think of the altar Paul found in Athens dedicated "To an Unknown God" (Acts 17:23).

But Christians affirm more than this. Christians affirm that we know God's very name because God has revealed it. God's name is so holy that some Jews, out of reverence, will not even speak it: YHWH (see Exodus 3:13–15). This is a term notoriously hard to translate—perhaps "I am who I am" or "I will be who I will be." We also know that Jesus called

God "Abba," "Father" (see Mark 14:36), and he bid us make bold to call God "Father" as well (see Luke 11:2, Matthew 6:9).

Starting, if you will, with the name of God ("I believe in God, the Father..."), Christian creeds articulate in concise, almost poetic form, some of the most fundamental of the saving and joyful truths that constitute the Christian faith. Such formulations have been around since the beginnings of Christianity.

Scripture

The New Testament contains passages considered creedal. Some give witness to affirmations about Jesus: that he is Lord (see Romans 10:9; Philippians 2:11) or Christ (see Mark 8:29; 1 John 2:22, 5:1). Others list basic teachings (see Hebrews 6:1–2). Still others are more narrative in form, as when Paul reminds Corinthian Christians: "For I handed on to you as of first importance what I also received: that Christ died for our sins in accordance with the Scriptures; that he was buried; that he was raised on the third day in accordance with the Scriptures; that he appeared to Cephas, then to the Twelve" (1 Corinthians 15:3–5; the list continues for another few verses).

These passages tell us that from the beginning, Christians reflected theologically on what God had done in Christ and, under the guidance of God's Spirit, formulated that reflection into basic affirmations of faith. We can see something of the process and fruits of that reflection in the account of resurrection appearances in 1 Corinthians 15. We can also consider what implications might follow for us.

1. The first Christian believers sought and found theological meaning in the events of Christ's life. His death on the cross, for example, could seem to be a tragic end to a failed life. Instead, it was understood as a purposeful act undertaken and endured "for our sins"—that is, as part of God's saving plan (see Hebrews 10:12; 1 Peter 3:18; Matthew 1:21; 26:28). We, too, can find spiritual and catechetical riches by theologically pondering each event of

Christ's life, for each is a mystery given to us from which we can draw life (see *Catechism of the Catholic Church*, nos. 512–521).

2. The first Christians sought and found theological meaning in their personal and collective experiences of seeing the risen Christ. We too can theologically reflect on our own life experiences, seeking to sense God's presence within them and to hear God's call.

3. The first Christians sought and found the theological meaning of these events by pondering and interpreting them not just according to their own lights, but specifically by the light of revelation, "in accordance with the Scriptures"—a phrase still used in the Creed (see Romans 1:1–2; Luke 24:25–27 and 32). This reminds us to make our own prayer and catechetical ministry as thoroughly biblical as possible.

4. In their theological pondering, early Christians recognized certain features of their Christian beliefs to be more primary or pivotal than others. Paul thus speaks of the Paschal Mystery of Christ's death and resurrection as being "of first importance" (see Romans 4:24–25; 8:34, and 14:9; 2 Corinthians 13:4). The Second Vatican Council took the same approach in speaking of the "hierarchy of truths"—the understanding that, among the truths of the faith, some are more foundational while others are derivative (see *Decree on Ecumenism*, n. 11). For example, to say that God is Creator is foundational; belief in angels derives from that. This is an important distinction for catechists to know and teach.

Liturgy

Creeds were used not only didactically, as tools of teaching, but also liturgically, first in the rite of baptism. In that context, they took an explicitly Trinitarian form based on Matthew 28:19–20. What we know as the Apostles' Creed was the baptismal creed of the Roman church.

Baptismal professions of faith are dialogical: the person being baptized is asked whether he or she believes what the church believes about Father, Son, and Spirit, and the person replies, "I do."

> What we know as the Apostles' Creed was the baptismal creed of the Roman church.

Something essential about the Christian faith can be seen here. Saint Paul tells us that "faith comes from what is heard" (Romans 10:17). That is to say, the Christian faith is not something I think up or think out for myself; rather, it comes to me as a given, something I encounter from outside, that opens me up to what is beyond my own conceiving—which I then continue to ponder so as to understand it more deeply and live it more authentically.

Further, we see in this dialogue that Christian faith is inherently social; I receive it from others who have come before me, who hand it on to me so that I in turn can accept it, enter into it, be formed by it, and live from it. Then it falls to me, in turn, to proclaim and hand it on to others so they also may hear and, by God's grace, accept and enter into these saving mysteries (see *Introduction to Christianity*, Joseph Cardinal Ratzinger, San Francisco, CA: Ignatius Press, 2004). Through this entire process, of course, faith remains always and first of all a gift and grace of God; we can believe only with the prior and sustaining help of the Holy Spirit (see CCC, n. 153).

Creeds did not become part of the Mass until the sixth century, first in the Christian East and later in the West, in Spain. Around the year 800, the Nicene-Constantinopolitan Creed, formulated at the Councils of Nicaea (325) and Constantinople (381), was introduced into the Mass in Gaul (France). It was first used in the Mass at Rome in the year 1014, on the occasion of Pope Benedict VIII's coronation of St. Henry II; it was part of the ritual of Mass in Henry's Germany, and he requested (indeed, insisted) on its use. Ever since, it has been in the Roman liturgy, and we say or sing it at Mass on Sundays still today. We do so both to respond to the word of God just heard in the readings and preached in the homily, and "to honor and confess the great mysteries of the faith...before the celebration of these mysteries in the Eucharist begins" (*General Instruction of the Roman Missal*, n. 67).

I Believe—We Believe

Creeds sometimes begin "I believe," and sometimes "We believe." Both forms are traditional and legitimate, manifesting different aspects of the dynamics of faith. On the one hand, "faith is a personal act... the free response of the human person to God who reveals himself" (*Compendium: Catechism of the Catholic Church*, n. 30). Each one of us must come to be able to say for herself or himself, with mind well informed and heart fully engaged, "I believe"—and to do so more and more knowingly, committedly, and joyfully each year. Preparing us to do this at Easter, when we renew our baptismal promises, is one of the chief purposes of Lent.

At the same time—or should we say, but first of all—faith is "an ecclesial act which expresses itself in the proclamation, 'We believe'" (*Compendium*, n. 30). As noted before, faith is something we receive as a gift from God, a gift that typically comes to us through the church. "It is the Church that believes first, and so bears, nourishes, and sustains my faith....It is through the Church that we receive faith and new life in Christ by Baptism" (CCC, n. 168). We acknowledge the priority of the church's faith and our own need, choice, privilege, and joy to enter and participate in it when we profess "We believe."

Using the Creeds

How can we use the creeds so that they have a life-giving effect for us? Here are a few simple suggestions.

1. Learn them by heart.

Memorize our two principal creeds: the Nicene-Constantinopolitan Creed that we usually say at Mass, and the Apostles' Creed that may also be used at Mass and is always prayed at the beginning of the Rosary.

As St. John Paul II said, "the blossoms, if we may call them that, of faith and piety do not grow in the desert places of a memory-less catechesis." He immediately went on to add that "what is essential is that the texts that are memorized must at the same time be taken in and gradually understood in depth, in order to become a source of Christian life on the personal level and the community level" (*On Catechesis in Our Time*, n. 55). Fostering this understanding-in-depth is the role of catechetical ministry.

2. Pray them.

Pope Benedict XVI tells us that the Creed served the early Christians "as a daily prayer not to forget the commitment they had undertaken in Baptism" (PF, n. 9). Today, when reciting or singing the Creed at Mass, we can take care to be conscious of what we are professing, *meaning* the words as an expression of our own faith and trust in God. Or, in personal prayer, take time to pray the words of the Creed in the manner of *lectio divina*. In such ways as these, we can give ourselves to prayer and let God use the words of the Creed to lead us to deeper, stronger faith.

3. Teach them.

Find a way in your catechetical ministry to teach the creeds. You may be able to do a unit on a Creed or a segment of a Creed. At least make sure to reference the Creed as you teach what you teach—Scripture (e.g., "in accordance with the Scriptures"), church ("I believe in one, holy, catholic and apostolic Church"), sacraments ("I confess one Baptism for the forgiveness of sins"), and so on. Doing so may help learners see how your topic has its place in the larger framework of the Christian faith; it can help them understand more fully what they are saying at Mass when they profess the Creed.

One idea is to invite students in a classroom or perhaps on a retreat to formulate their own "personal" profession of faith (in an age-appropriate way). This can then be a way to help them become reflective, conscious, and articulate about their own way of understanding and expressing the faith that they hold and the faith that holds them.

If students have formulated a creed and would like to use it in a prayer service for the group, it is appropriate to do so. Nevertheless, it is not appropriate for use in a Mass, because the Mass or the Liturgy of the Hours is never just that gathered assembly's prayer; it is always a participation in the liturgy of the church—indeed, in the liturgy of heaven (see CCC, nos. 1090, 1137-1139). Just as we always read only Scripture at Mass and not any other reading, however personally meaningful to a particular person or community, so also we do not change the Creed when celebrating Mass. Rather, we honor and share in the profession of the church's faith hallowed by generations of use, and let ourselves be formed in faith by it.

Using this Common Language

Creedal formulas have been part of the church's life from the beginning, and they continue to play an essential role in the church today, for "they permit one to express, assimilate, celebrate, and share together with others the truth of the faith through a common language" (*Compendium*, n. 31). Through our use of this common language of faith, may we seek to grow together in faith and in love for God and one another.

Your Thoughts

1 What is my experience of praying the Creed during the liturgy or at other times? Do I pray the Creed—or am I simply saying the words? What is the difference between "praying" and "saying" the Creed?

_____

_____

_____

2 How can I use the Creeds so that they have a life-giving effect in my life?

_____

_____

_____

Try This

First, spend quality time reflecting on the Creed. Then put the Creed into your own words. What difference does it offer you for praying the Creed during Mass?

The SCRIPTURES *and* SPIRITUALITY *of* CATECHISTS

FR. DONALD SENIOR, CP

To transmit to one's students a love of the Scriptures is possible only when the catechist, too, has a deep love of the Bible and draws on the Scripture for his or her own spiritual nourishment and inspiration.

I n *Word of God (Verbum Domini)*, Pope Benedict XVI's remarkable exhortation in response to the Synod on the Scriptures in the Life and Ministry of the Church—Benedict emphasized the central role of the Bible in the catechetical ministry of the church. It is not simply a matter of the content of the Scriptures informing the church's catechesis but the profound impact that the Bible can have on the spirituality of the catechists themselves. As he notes, the church's catechesis "must be permeated by the mindset, the spirit and the outlook of the Bible and the Gospels…" (VD, n. 74).

To make his point, Pope Benedict recalled the beautiful story at the end of Luke's gospel in which the two disciples on the road to Emmaus have their sadness and disappointment transformed into joy as the risen

Christ himself, beginning with Moses and all the prophets, interprets the Scriptures for them. "Were not our hearts burning within us while he spoke to us on the way and opened the Scriptures to us?" (Luke 24:32). What catechist would not dream of having his or her students say the same as they look back upon what they had learned from their encounter with the Word of God?

To transmit to one's students a love of the Scriptures is possible only when the catechist, too, has a deep love of the Bible and draws on the Scripture for his or her own spiritual nourishment and inspiration. The church has often compared the Scriptures to the Eucharist itself. Just as we are nourished by the Body and Blood of Christ in the Eucharist, so, too, does the Word of God that comes to us in the Scriptures become like living bread that can fill our very being with new life.

How can one gain a deeper love of God's word? Drawing on *Word of God* and other sources of the church's collective wisdom, let me suggest a few ways.

A Habit of the Heart

First and foremost, anyone who wants to be steeped in the Scriptures and draw life from them has to develop a habit of actually reading the Bible. This does not mean we have to plow through the Bible from beginning to end—although that is not a bad idea! But we can make it a point to read more accessible passages on a frequent, if not daily, basis.

The gospels, Paul's letters, the stories of Genesis and Exodus, the writings of Isaiah and the prophets, the Psalms: These are fairly familiar ground for most of us. But what a difference it makes to read slowly, thoughtfully, prayerfully—on a regular basis—passages from these books of the Bible. Many Catholics use the daily readings in the Lectionary as their guide through the biblical world—each day sampling the texts that are heard at the Eucharist by millions of Christians around the world.

There are innumerable publications that provide attractive and inexpensive booklets that contain the daily readings and prayers of the Eucharist. Three good examples are *Living with Christ* (livingwithchrist.us);

Give Us This Day (giveusthisday.org); and *Magnificat* (catholiccompany.com/magnificat). Some of these offer daily prayers and reflections in an online format.

And, yes, there are several good apps with the Lectionary readings for those who want to put them on their electronic devices.

Appreciating the Whole Story

The Bible, we know, is not a single, uniform book. Rather, it is a collection of books with a variety of literary forms composed over different periods of history and emerging from ancient cultures very different from our own. It is easy enough to get submerged in the details, and a lay person who has not had an opportunity for extended study of the Scriptures often may feel lost in the weeds.

While the prayerful reading of individual passages is at the heart of the matter, it is also important to keep the big picture in mind. The Bible as we now have it charts what we could call "the history of salvation." This is the great saga of faith that frames the Scriptures and gives overall meaning to our world and its destiny. I sometimes think of the major components of that sacred history as humanity's life cycle:

- Genesis tells the remote origins of our world and our ancestors, beginning with the creation stories and on into the drama of the patriarchs Abraham and Jacob and Moses.
- The Exodus stories take us to the moment of the birth of Israel as it emerges from the slavery of Egypt and begins its life journey toward freedom.
- The desert wandering that we read about in the books of Exodus, Leviticus, and Deuteronomy is a strange and important interlude in the biblical saga, not unlike the turbulent and formative time of one's adolescence. There is rebellion and experimentation during this testing period, but it is also a time when Israel is formed as God's people and given the covenant with God.
- We can think of the period recounted in books like Joshua, Judges,

Samuel, Kings, and Chronicles as the "maturation" of Israel—its middle age, if you like—when it took possession of its land and ultimately built the monarchy and its social institutions.

- But, strangely, it was right at this moment of its greatest strength that Israel began to lose its way, and its founding ideals were forgotten and violated. There then comes that part of the Bible when the disturbing and challenging voices of the prophets—Amos, Hosea, Isaiah, Jeremiah, and so on—are heard, calling Israel back to its defining values and allegiance with God.

- And then all seems lost and diminished for Israel as it experiences deportation and exile—not unlike the period of aging in the human life cycle, when many of the things we counted on seem to break down. So many of the Psalms and part of the prophetic books lament Israel's loss and cry out for God's help.

- And that brings the story of Israel to a new moment, one of greater serenity and peace—as it returns to its homeland and no longer puts its trust in mere human institutions but longs for God to come and redeem Israel. Here the books of Ezra and Nehemiah, parts of Ezekiel, and later biblical books speak about the hopes of Israel for God's coming reign.

From the viewpoint of Christian faith, the decisive chapter of this story is found in the New Testament, where the word of God that has coursed throughout Israel's history now becomes flesh in the person and mission of Jesus Christ. Jesus, the one sent by the Father, brings the fullness of life and hope to our world.

The story of Jesus and the reflections upon his death and resurrection that are the focus of the New Testament writings do not negate or render obsolete the Old Testament writings. Rather, for the Christian reader of the Bible, the story of Israel takes on new meaning and coherence in the light of Christ.

Reading the Scriptures from this overall vantage point helps us keep track of how each individual component of the Bible fits into the story of salvation. And that story of salvation should also be deep in the consciousness and life story of the one entrusted with teaching the Gospel to others.

The Scriptures as Mirror

Some interpreters of the Bible have suggested that we can approach the Scriptures either as a "window" or as a "mirror." Reading the Bible as a "window" means that our interest is primarily in the history and context that lies behind a particular biblical story or passage: e.g., What really happened in the crossing of the Red Sea and where was the original Mt. Sinai located? Or how many gallons did those stone jars hold at the wedding feast of Cana and who were the Sadducees?

> Some interpreters of the Bible have suggested that we can approach the Scriptures either as a "window" or a "mirror."

While such historical and contextual questions are legitimate and important, the approach we are talking about here is more like reading the Scriptures as if they are a "mirror"—that is, the focus is on the relationship between the biblical text and the life of the reader. What does this biblical passage mean for me—or for us? How does my experience or our experiences relate to the biblical passage? How does one illumine the other?

Most people of faith turn to the Scriptures with this kind of interest in mind. When Moses tells the people of Israel that they should be attentive to the needs of the widow, the orphan, and the sojourner (see Deuteronomy 10:18), what does that mean for me today? When Jesus tells Peter to forgive "not seven times but seventy-seven times" (Matthew 18:22), what light does that throw on my struggles with my spouse or my children?

Here is where a habit of prayerfully reading the Bible can work its way deeply into our life. Sometimes the words and images and stories of the Bible give us the right words or images to understand and express our experience. For example, God's verdict in the creation story of Genesis 1 about the intrinsic goodness of the world he created expresses our commitment to respect the environment. Jesus' anguished words from the cross—"My God, my God, why have you forsaken me?" (Mark 15:34; Matthew 27:46)—enable us to express our anguish and confusion at times of deep suffering. Jesus' reassuring words to his disciples—"Do not let your hearts be troubled…I am going to prepare a place for you…" (John 14:1, 2)—have brought comfort to those who mourn the loss of loved ones at countless funerals. The parables of the Rich Man and Lazarus or the Publican and the Sinner have made indelible marks on our literature and often come to mind to guide us through moral dilemmas. The gospel stories of Jesus' calling his first disciples and sending them out on mission have forged the language of Christian vocation throughout the centuries. Such examples could be multiplied without end.

Heart and Head

Illuminating our lives and our experiences with the words and images of the Scriptures is, indeed, a habit of the Christian heart. We need our heads, too! Interpretation of the Bible is not a matter of a personal whim; over time, all of us need the wisdom of the church's teaching and the good sense of other Christians to help us keep on an even keel. Yet the incredibly rich and beautiful metaphors, images, and stories of the Bible belong to us and—like exquisite poetry or great literature—can help us find the right words to express our deepest longings and strongest hopes.

Making frequent and prayerful reading and study of Scripture a habit of the heart, keeping in mind the overall biblical story as the framework for understanding particular books or passage of the Bible, and allowing the Scriptures to illumine our own experience and thereby finding in the Scriptures the words and images for our deepest human longings: these are some of the ways we too might feel our hearts burning within us on our journey of faith.

Your Thoughts

1 Do I bring the Scriptures to life every day? If not, what are the challenges I face? (Be specific.)

_____

_____

_____

2 How often is my heart burning within me when I prayerfully engage the Scriptures, either for strengthening my spiritual life or awakening a love for the word of God in the lives of my students?

_____

_____

Try This

To deepen your appreciation of Scriptures, read Pope Benedict XVI's apostolic letter *Word of God*. What new insights do you receive that may help you rediscover a love for the Scriptures or help you stimulate a love for the Scriptures in your students?

IMPLEMENTING
the CATECHISM

DANIEL S. MULHALL

The word catechism *is applied to a written work that presents a full summary of beliefs that is created as a means of passing on those beliefs to others.*

From the earliest days of the church, efforts have been made to present the beliefs of the faith clearly and completely. Much of the New Testament can be seen as catechetical, as can many of the writings of early church fathers such as Origen and Augustine.

A Brief History of the Catechism of the Catholic Church

Types of catechisms: Over the centuries, there have been many types of catechisms. Some have been written as narratives, attempting to create a story of the faith that attracts believers to the beauty that resides there. Others, like the *Baltimore Catechism*, are written in a question-and-answer format that is designed to promote in children the memorization of specific beliefs. Some catechisms have been written for the benefit of clergy and teachers, to ensure that they have at their fingertips the completeness of faith. Others have been written for use by the uneducated and the young, that they may learn the church's beliefs in a simplified language.

The *Catechism of the Catholic Church* (CCC) is formally known as a "major" catechism. It was written to be a "sure guide" to the faith for those who teach the church's message and for those who wish to develop "minor" catechisms to be used by children and those seeking initial understanding. The CCC is written in a narrative form and does not use the question-and-answer format.

The audience: Catechisms are always written for particular audiences at particular times in history. While revelation was completed in Jesus Christ, and the church's faith doesn't change over time, the language in which the faith is expressed does develop and change, as do the ways in which people use catechisms. Thus, it is important that official expressions of the faith—catechisms—be updated regularly so that the message of faith can be shared in such a way that people can understand it more fully.

St. John XXIII was aware of the tremendous changes that were taking place in the world following the Second World War. So he called on the fathers of the Second Vatican Council to guard and present Christian doctrine in such a way that it was most accessible to the world—Catholics, other Christians, and all people of faith. The documents of the Second Vatican Council expressed the faith of the church clearly for the new age. While the development of an official catechism was discussed at the council, the bishops decided not to create a new catechism at that time, choosing instead to let the church live with the council's teaching and make them into a living reality. So it wasn't until 1985 that the church gave serious consideration to the creation of such a catechism.

The **Catechism of the Catholic Church** *proposed and written:* The CCC was first proposed at a synod of bishops gathered to reflect on the twentieth anniversary of the conclusion of the Second Vatican Council. Cardinal Bernard Law of Boston made the proposal that a new universal catechism be developed to replace the then still official *Catechism of the Council of Trent*, which was created in 1566. Recognizing that such a work would be helpful, the bishops at the synod accepted the proposal, and St. John Paul II approved the CCC's creation.

The CCC was written by a commission of scholars appointed by St. John Paul II. The scholars began their work in November 1986 and completed it in February 1992. The Holy Father approved the text and released the first "provisional reference text" to the world in October of that year to show that the CCC was a product of the Second Vatican Council, not an addendum to or in opposition to the teachings of the council. The first official English translation of the provisional CCC was published in 1994. Because the original CCC was written in French, it had to be translated into Latin, the official language of the church. The official Latin edition (the "typical edition") was published on August 15, 1997, and was translated into English later in 1997. The second edition of the CCC published by the United States Conference of Catholic Bishops (USCCB) also contains a Glossary and *Index Analyticus* that were published in 2000.

For a fuller history of catechisms and catechesis, go to usccb.org and search "Informative Dossier on the Catechism of the Catholic Church."

The Purpose of the Catechism

As a major catechism, the CCC was written as "a sure and authentic reference text for teaching Catholic doctrine and particularly for preparing local catechisms" (*Deposit of Faith*). For this reason, the CCC presents the story of faith as an unfolding of the story of God's revelation to humanity that was fulfilled in Jesus Christ and continues to be lived by the church, guided by the Holy Spirit. As stated in *Deposit of Faith*, "the contents are often presented in a new way in order to respond to the questions of our age."

Because it is a reference text, the CCC was created to guide the development of other catechetical materials that would be used with specific audiences. To facilitate this usage, the USCCB has created a subcommittee of bishops that reviews catechetical texts to ensure that the texts are in conformity with the *Catechism*, meaning that what is presented in the text is complete and accurate according to the CCC. The subcommittee reviews only those texts voluntarily submitted, and reviews only in relation to the CCC. The subcommittee does not "approve" text and makes no statement about the text's methodology or appropriateness for use by any group.

Finally, the conformity statement does not replace the need for an *imprimatur* or approval of use by the local bishop. For more information on the work of this subcommittee, visit usccb.org and search "subcommittee on catechism."

The Four Parts of the *Catechism*

The CCC is organized into four parts:

- "Part One: The Profession of Faith" takes the key themes from the Apostles' Creed and explains them.
- "Part Two: The Celebration of the Christian Mystery" explains the church's liturgy and Sacraments.
- "Part Three: Life in Christ" examines how we are to live guided by the Holy Spirit, the Beatitudes, and the Ten Commandments.
- "Part Four: Christian Prayer" examines the role of prayer in our lives and how we are to pray. It includes a reflection on the Lord's Prayer.

These four parts are often called the "four pillars" of the Catholic faith. The CCC contains numerous footnotes, along with references to the teaching from the church's storehouse of traditions and from authoritative Catholic statements. The CCC also is cross-referenced to itself; numbers in margins indicate where else in the book a particular topic is addressed.

While not one of the organizing principles of the CCC, sacred Scripture is an essential component of its makeup. Paragraphs numbered 101–141 present a spiritual exegesis on Scripture and show how the church's Tradition flows from Scripture. This treatment of Scripture is taken from *Dei verbum*, the Second Vatican Council's *Dogmatic Constitution on Divine Revelation*, which emphasized that Scripture should be "read and interpreted in light of the same Spirit by whom it was written" (*Dei verbum*, n. 12). In addition, Scripture is used continuously throughout the CCC and referenced repeatedly.

Using the *Catechism*

Because the CCC was created to guide the development of other texts, it was not intended to be used as a general catechetical text. That doesn't mean that it can't or shouldn't be used in this way—especially for adults—only that one shouldn't assume that the CCC replaces other catechetical resources.

Like catechisms, catechetical resources are developed for particular audiences at particular times. Catechetical materials for first-graders who are just beginning to read will be different from those created for twelfth-graders who can think abstractly and study a topic thoroughly. While it is important that materials for all learners are accurate and complete—which the CCC helps to ensure—they must also be created with the developmental needs of the learner in mind.

So, if you are not to teach directly from the CCC, how can you use it most effectively? Here are a number of suggestions:

Check your textbook references to the CCC: Most catechetical textbooks are designed to teach certain segments of the CCC. These segments are frequently listed in the teacher's edition, along with commentaries on the CCC written with the teacher of a certain grade level in mind. By all means, when you come upon these references, look them up and read them. Check out the footnotes and references and check other sections of the CCC that pertain to the topic. Become as familiar as you can with the contents of the CCC: the better you know it, the easier it will be for you to interpret it faithfully to those you teach.

Study the CCC on your own: When you come upon a topic about the faith that you don't understand, go to the *Catechism* and study what it says. Many dioceses encourage their catechists to use the *Catechism* as a source of reflection and meditation so that they can continue to grow as persons of faith. You might pick a particular section for a season of the year, such as Advent or Lent, and then read and reflect on one or two paragraphs of the CCC each day. You will be surprised at how this will help you grow in your understanding of the faith.

Pray with the CCC: The CCC also provides a wonderful vehicle to guide and shape prayer. In addition to the fourth part, which teaches about prayer, there are opportunities throughout the *Catechism* for the reader to stop and pray upon the mystery that is presented there.

Use the CCC as a reference tool: Have it at hand anytime you prepare or teach a lesson. If someone asks a question, invite that person to look up the topic in the one sure source for what the church believes and teaches.

A Gift to the Church

The *Catechism of the Catholic Church* is a wonderful gift to the church. The more it is used, the greater the gift becomes.

Your Thoughts

1 What has been my past experience with the church's catechisms, e.g., *Baltimore Catechism?* What impact did that experience have on my forming a personal relationship with Jesus or on discovering my faith at a deeper level?

_____

_____

2 What have I understood the role of the *Catechism of the Catholic Church* to be in the church, in my life, and in my ministry as a catechist? What has been my experience with reading, reflecting, praying, and using the CCC as a reference in my catechetical ministry? (Be specific.)

_____

_____

Try This

Plan for an intentional, conscious journey through the CCC. Select articles out of each section of the four parts and allow them to be the portal for rediscovering your faith.

MARY: DISCIPLE
and WOMAN *of* FAITH

FR. BERTRAND BUBY, SM

Even though the word disciple is never used directly in association with Mary in the gospels, she is, according to the criteria for discipleship,… a faithful disciple of Jesus.

Mary, the mother of Jesus, is esteemed in the Gospel of Luke as "most blessed…among women" (1:42). We are accustomed to celebrating her memory and person in the solemnities and feasts dedicated to her. The months of May and October are considered months in which she is called to mind through our devotions as well as through the Liturgy of the Word. The forty-six Masses dedicated to her are often celebrated on Saturdays when there is no special Mass dedicated to a saint.

In this reflection, we want to learn more about Mary as a disciple of Jesus and a woman of faith. Perhaps the following questions will help us meditate and reflect upon Mary, the faithful disciple of the Lord:

- How does Mary offer us an example of discipleship in the gospels?
- What are the characteristics and criteria of discipleship given to us

in the inspired words of the New Testament?

- Is Mary able to be called the faithful and perfect disciple of the Lord?

Our theological and scriptural reflection will be guided by the above three questions to see how Mary is a disciple of the Lord and how she meets the criteria for discipleship.

Mary in Scripture and Tradition

The gospels are our primary source for reflecting on and responding to these questions. Mary is mentioned in all four gospels and in the Acts of the Apostles. There is also a long tradition of seeing Mary and the church in the symbolism of the woman clothed with the sun in the twelfth chapter of the Book of Revelation (Apocalypse).

Even though the word *disciple* is never used directly in association with Mary in the gospels, she is, according to the criteria for discipleship—and through a theological reflection upon the Marian texts of the New Testament—a faithful disciple of Jesus. In addition to her being called simply Mary, the mother of Jesus, virgin, and woman, we see Mary fulfilling the call to be a disciple.

By reading the Scriptures in a holistic and contextual way, we certainly will be led to call her a disciple of Jesus. In turn, this will lead us to look at our own call from Jesus to be his disciples—not only after the example of the saintly Apostles and disciples of the past but also in our own circumstances today.

The word *disciple* is almost exclusively used in the gospels. Paul does not use it in his epistles nor is it found in the other writings except in the Acts of the Apostles. Luke calls to discipleship all believing Christians who are members in the emerging communities of faith and are dedicated to the person, words, and works of Jesus of Nazareth, the son of Mary.

Because the word for "disciple" is found 261 times in the gospels and Acts, we have sufficient textual evidence for discovering the key characteristics of discipleship. From this evidence we may be led to see Mary as the faithful disciple for our call to follow Jesus.

The word for "follow" (*akolouthein*) is linked to the calling of a disciple. It means "a companion who goes behind a teacher or goes after the teacher." The word indicating this following is *disciple* (*mathetes* from *manthano*: to learn, to be familiar with or accustomed to someone or something). Depending on the translation that is referenced, both words—*following* and *disciple*—are rarely found in the Old Testament; only one text shows use of the word *disciple* (see 1 Chronicles 25:8).

To Be a Disciple

The seven characteristics and criteria for becoming a disciple are:

1. It is always Jesus who initiates the call to follow him and become his disciple (see cf. Mark 1:17; 2:14).
2. A disciple of Jesus is called to break totally from his or her past. This is compared to a seed falling into the ground and dying (see John 12:24). In Mark, we have the earliest reference to such a separation in the words of Jesus intimating that the one who does the will of God is mother, sister, and brother to him (see Mark 3:31–35; also Mark 1:17; Luke 14:26). Discipleship is a call to enter into the Paschal Mystery of Christ, which we do at each Eucharist.
3. Our ordinary way of thinking and acting is changed into thinking the thoughts of God and Jesus. Some customary values are to be radically set aside in this following of Jesus (see Mark 10:41–45). The call makes demands of us, makes possible the break with our past, and gives us a new vision and future.
4. A disciple is a person who experiences life with Jesus and has a lifelong relationship to the very person of Jesus.
5. As a disciple of Jesus, one is sent out to witness to him, to become a "missionary" (*apostoloi, apostellein*), that is, to announce the Good News, which is Jesus himself.
6. According to Luke, in Acts of the Apostles, all disciples are believ-

ing Christians who are sent out to bring Jesus and his message to everyone. Matthew, too, tells us: "Go, therefore, and make disciples of all the nations" (28:19). Discipleship becomes a universal call to holiness and witnessing to Jesus.

7. A personal relationship and experience of Jesus leads our discipleship into the intimacy that the Beloved Disciple had with Jesus and then with Mary. Phillip Mueller states: "The one who, like the Beloved Disciple, rests at Jesus' side will receive a deeper view of reality and of the meaning of discipleship—wherever such a path may lead" (*Theological Digest*, Summer 2010, p. 157). Thus, discipleship is a prophetic call to be one with Jesus. Paul expresses it in this way: "For to me life is Christ" (Philippians 1:21).

Having analyzed the criteria for being a disciple, we now turn to the four gospels and the Acts of the Apostles to see how Mary is a disciple of the Lord. Chronologically, we move from Mark to Matthew to Luke to John, then to the Acts of the Apostles.

> [Jesus'] mother, brothers, and sisters are those who accept the call of discipleship because they, too, are called to do the will of the Father.

In Mark: Mary Enters the Mystery

In the Gospel according to Mark, the cost of discipleship is seen in the passage where Jesus is sought out by his mother and his relatives (see Mark 3:31–35). Jesus has left his home in Nazareth and has begun his active ministry. In this passage, Mary will learn that the blood relationship she has as mother of Jesus is asked to be transformed into the same mission that Jesus has—which will have no ties to his natural family.

Mary will have to accept this as his disciple who seeks, with him, to do the will of the Father. In Mark, Jesus has no father figure other than God working through him in his mission of teaching, preaching, and healing. His mother, brothers, and sisters are those who accept the call of discipleship because they, too, are called to do the will of the Father.

Mary enters this mystery through her silence, which will lead her to experience the Paschal Mystery and the radical cost of discipleship that Mark's theology requires. All who have faith in Jesus and follow his call will undergo what Jesus will experience in his sufferings, death, and resurrection.

In Matthew: Mary Remains Ever Faithful

The Infancy Narrative in the Gospel according to Matthew (chapters 1 and 2) presents Mary as virgin and mother respectively. Matthew points out the role of Joseph as the foster father and protector of Mary and her child (see Matthew 1:16–25; Matthew 2). Matthew closely follows what Mark says about Mary but gives it a slightly different slant in the description of Mary and the brethren approaching him.

Jesus is now teaching those surrounding him about discipleship. In Matthew's gospel, we discover Mary as the only one who would be with Jesus through the stages of his conception, birth, and active ministry; and in his sufferings, death, and resurrection. Jesus' "silent years" are under Mary's and Joseph's tutelage and care. Jesus is trained in the work of a *tekton* (a builder, a carpenter) by Joseph, his legal father (see Matthew 1:18–25).

Mary shows that her following of her son is a lifelong commitment to him—not only as mother but also as a faithful disciple. No one enjoyed the thirty-plus years with Jesus more than his mother, Mary. It was a permanent, constant, and single-hearted commitment to Jesus through her virginity, her motherhood, and her discipleship. She exemplifies what Jesus teaches in the Beatitudes, and indeed is a blessed and happy person (*makaria* in Matthew 5:1–11). Without losing anything, Matthew builds upon what Mark teaches us about Mary and gives it a positive thrust.

In Luke: Mary Reverses the Standards

The Gospel according to Luke paints the most beautiful and complete portrait of Mary's discipleship in the Annunciation (see Luke 1:26–38), where she is called by God and overshadowed by the Holy Spirit to be the virginal-mother disciple. In her visit to Elizabeth and in her song of praise called the Magnificat (see Luke 1:46–55), Mary is active in her role as disciple. She gives us the spirit of what a disciple is.

We see Mary as radically reversing the standards of the temporal-order world into a perspective of social justice and peace. She does this through her strong commitment to her call and through her transparency and openness to her vocation. Mary participates in the history of salvation as a creative and active agent of discipleship.

In John and Acts: Mary Surrenders, Responds

The Gospel according to John continues to develop the discipleship of Mary through what happens at Cana and at Calvary (see John 2:1–12; John 19:27–28).

If the Beloved Disciple leaned upon the breast of Jesus, Jesus leaned upon the breast of Mary in his earliest years. The Beloved Disciple cannot be separated from Mary. He will take her into his intimacy (*ta idia* in John 19:27). She, like the Evangelist John and the mysterious person of the Beloved Disciple, is the guarantor of the content of the gospel, which is the call to become and continue to the end as a faith-filled disciple. Mary does this while standing at the foot of the cross as Jesus severs his last bond with her and entrusts her to the intimate care and friendship with the Beloved Disciple, who is a model figure with her as the woman of faith.

At Cana, Mary shows us her absolute commitment and trust in Jesus; at Calvary she stands there at the foot of the cross. She is with him in this last hour (his passion and death). "What is decisive is whether one devotes one's entire person to following Jesus and remaining faithful to him. What is important is to surrender solely to Jesus. In the end, which path Jesus leads someone along is not important" (Mueller, *Theological Digest*, Summer 2010, p. 62).

Faith and trust in the person of Jesus, the Word made flesh, is what Mary shows us at Cana (*pisteuein eis Iesoun*). At Calvary, love (*agape*) is what she shows us through her perseverance and intimacy in her relationship to Jesus as his first Beloved Disciple.

In the Acts of the Apostles, Mary is seen for the last time in the New Testament. She once again waits for the coming of the Holy Spirit upon her and her new spiritual family gathered in the Upper Room. They are now experiencing the new birth of Jesus through the action of the Holy Spirit. Mary models for them how to respond to their call as his disciples. Luke will now be able to use the word *disciple* in reference to all who follow Jesus.

> Mary shows all of us the way that leads to this universal call in which we all share in her mission of bringing Jesus to others.

Mary shows all of us the way that leads to this universal call in which we all share in her mission of bringing Jesus to others. She has given us the persuasive and graced command to "do whatever he tells you" (John 2:5).

Closing Prayer

Lord Jesus, we gather in spirit at the foot of the cross with your mother and faithful disciple Mary, and with the Beloved Disciple whom you loved. We ask your pardon for our sins, which are the cause of your death. We thank you for remembering us in that hour of salvation, and for giving us Mary as our mother and our model in discipleship.

Holy Virgin, take us under your protection and open us to the action of the Holy Spirit.

Beloved Disciple, obtain for us the grace of taking Mary into our lives, as you did, and of assisting her in her mission.

May the Father, the Son, and the Holy Spirit be glorified in all places through the Immaculate Virgin Mary.

Your Thoughts

1 What is my relationship to Mary, the mother of Jesus? Does this relationship strengthen my intimacy with the person of Jesus? How? Why? (Be specific.)

_____

_____

_____

2 What does this chapter say about the meaning of discipleship? Does this relate to my previous understanding? How do I live out discipleship in my life as a catechist? (Be specific.)

_____

_____

_____

Try This

Using the biblical references in this chapter, explore each of the gospels for a more in-depth understanding of Mary's presence in the life of Jesus and the first disciples.

ABOUT THE CONTRIBUTORS

General Editor
Sr. Angela Ann Zukowski, MHSH, DMin, is the Director of the Institute for Pastoral Initiatives and Professor in the Department of Religious Studies of the University of Dayton. She is a member of the Mission Helpers of the Sacred Heart (Towson, MD).

Chapter 1
Sr. Janet Schaeffler, OP, is a facilitator of days of reflection, retreats, workshops, presentations, and online classes for the University of Dayton and Boston College. She was on the four-member team who wrote the Leader's Guide to accompany *Our Hearts Were Burning Within Us* (Washington, DC: USCCB, 1999).

Chapter 2
Sr. Angela Ann Zukowski, MHSH, DMin (See General Editor.)

Chapter 3
Most Reverend Bishop Charles Jason Gordon was ordained Bishop of Bridgetown (Barbados) and Kingstown (St. Vincent and the Grenadines) in September 2011. He is the Communications Chairperson for the Antilles Episcopal Conference.

Chapter 4
William H. Johnston, PhD, is Associate Professor; Acting Committee Chair of Masters Programs in Theological Studies and Pastoral Ministry at the University of Dayton. He has held parish and archdiocesan catechetical positions, directed a diocesan ministry formation program, and chaired the board of NALM.

Chapter 5
Fr. Donald Senior, CP, STL, STD, is President Emeritus of Catholic Theological Union in Chicago, where he is also Professor of New Testament. Fr. Senior is past President of the Catholic Biblical Association of America and of the Association of Theological Schools of the United States and Canada.

Chapter 6
Daniel S. Mulhall, MA, currently serves as the Director of Professional Development and Hispanic Catechesis for RCL Benziger. He holds a master's degree in Theology from the Catholic University of America (1979) and a master's degree in Adult Christian Community Development from Regis University (1989).

Chapter 7
Fr. Bertrand Buby, SM, STD, was ordained in 1964. He teaches at the International Marian Research Institute at the University of Dayton. He has published a three-volume work titled *Mary of Galilee* (New York: Alba House, 1994).

RECOMMENDED RESOURCES

**The following are available from the
United States Conference of Catholic Bishops
or your local Catholic bookstore**

National Directory for Catechesis. Washington, DC:
United States Conference of Catholic Bishops, 2005

General Directory for Catechesis. Washington, DC. Congregation for
the Clergy. United States Conference of Catholic Bishops, 1997

New American Bible, Revised Edition.
United States Conference of Catholic Bishops, 2011

Catechism of the Catholic Church. Vatican City. Second Edition. 1997

Available online at www.vatican.va

The Door of Faith (Porta Fidei)

Word of God (Verbum Domini)

Constitution on the Sacred Liturgy (Sacrosanctum Concilium)

Charity in Truth (Caritas in Veritate)

The Development of Peoples (Populorum Progressio)

On Catechesis in Our Time (Catechesi Tradendae)

Dogmatic Constitution on Divine Revelation (Dei Verbum)

Decree on Ecumenism (Unitatis Redintegratio)

Called to Be a Catechist

INSPIRATION AND PROFESSIONAL GROWTH

Titles Now Available

The Role of the Catechist
9781627851558

The Vocation of the Catechist
9781627852876

Communicating the Faith
9781627852883

Breaking Open the Scriptures
9781627852890

Celebrating the Sacraments
9781627852920

Fostering Spirituality
9781627852906

Pondering the Parables
9781627852913

Discovering Discipleship
9781627852937

Abiding in Prayer
9781627852944

Practicing the Beatitudes
9781627852951

TO ORDER CALL 1-800-321-0411
OR VISIT WWW.TWENTYTHIRDPUBLICATIONS.COM

TWENTY-THIRD
PUBLICATIONS
A division of Bayard, Inc.